SHIRLEY WILLIS was born in Glasgow. She has worked as an illustrator, designer and editor, mainly on books for children.

BETTY ROOT was the Director of the Reading and Language Information Centre at the University of Reading for over twenty years. She has worked on numerous children's books, both fiction and non-fiction.

PETER LAFFERTY is a former secondary school science teacher. Since 1985 he has been a full-time author of science and technology books for children and family audiences. He has edited and contributed to many scientific encyclopedias and dictionaries.

EDITORS: KAREN BARKER SMITH
STEPHANIE COLE
TECHNICAL CONSULTANT: PETER LAFFERTY
LANGUAGE CONSULTANT: BETTY ROOT

PUBLISHED IN GREAT BRITAIN IN 2002 BY
BOOK HOUSE, AN IMPRINT OF
THE SALARIYA BOOK COMPANY LTD,
25 MARLBOROUGH PLACE, BRIGHTON, BN1 1UB
© THE SALARIYA BOOK COMPANY LTD MMII

ISBN 1 904194 05 2

VISIT THE SALARIYA BOOK COMPANY AT:
www.SALARIYA.COM
www.BOOK-HOUSE.co.UK

PRINTED IN ITALY
PRINTED ON PAPER FROM SUSTAINABLE FORESTS.

WHIZ KIDS

CONTENTS

Wherever you see this sign, ask an adult to help you.

WHIZ KIDS

TELL ME WHY THE MOON CHANGES SHAPE

Written and illustrated by
SHIRLEY WILLIS

BOOK HOUSE

HOW FAR IS THE MOON?

The moon is our nearest neighbour in space but it is a long way from Earth.

THE MOON IS ABOUT 385,000 KM AWAY!

It takes a rocket
3 days and 3 nights
to reach the moon.

A BALLOON ROCKET

You will need: A long balloon
A straw
A ball of string
Sticky tape
Scissors

1. Shorten the straw by cutting it in two. (Ask an adult to help.)
2. Thread the string through the straw and tie it onto something high so that the other end touches the floor.
3. Blow up the balloon and hold it tightly to keep the air in.
4. Ask a friend to tape the balloon to the straw (as shown).
5. Pull the string down so that it is tight.
6. Let go of the balloon. You have lift off!

WHOOSH!

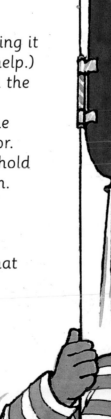

HOW BIG IS THE MOON?

The moon measures 10,921 km around its widest part. It is much smaller than Earth.

THE BIG BALL IS LIKE EARTH!

THE SMALL BALL IS LIKE THE MOON!

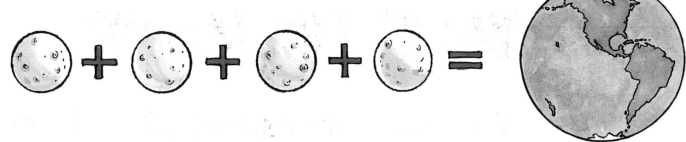

Earth measures 40,000 km around its widest part. It is four times as big as the moon.

9

HOW OLD IS THE MOON?

The moon is 4.6 billion years old. It is as old as Earth.

The moon was there long before dinosaurs lived on Earth.

WHY DOES THE MOON SHINE?

The brightest thing in the sky
is the Sun. It is made of
burning gases that
give off heat and light.

The moon has no light
of its own. It shines because
it reflects the light
from the Sun.

12

Light from the Sun bounces off the moon. This is called reflection. Moonlight is a reflection of the Sun's light.

MOONLIGHT IS REFLECTED LIGHT!

MOON

SUN

13

WHAT GOES AROUND AND AROUND?

The moon travels around
Earth all the time
– it is never still.

The moon's journey
around Earth
is called an orbit.

Earth

moon

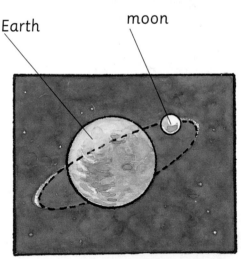

The moon goes
around Earth
like this.

14

WHY DOES THE MOON CHANGE SHAPE?

We see the moon when it is lit by the Sun.

Sometimes only part of the moon is sunlit, so we only see part of it. This makes the moon's shape look different each night.

THE DIFFERENT SHAPES WE SEE ARE CALLED THE PHASES OF THE MOON!

LOOK AT THE MOON
– WHAT DO YOU SEE?

When the Sun lights up a small part of the moon...

this is what the moon looks like to us.

The Sun lights up different parts of the moon as the moon orbits Earth. We only see the part that is sunlit. The rest of the moon is dark – we cannot see it.
The moon's shape changes because a new part is sunlit each night.

17

WHERE DOES THE MOON GO?

The moon does not go
away in the morning.
Sometimes we can see
it in the daytime, but it
is easy to see it at night
when the sky is dark.

Some nights, the moon shines brightly. Some nights, it is hidden behind clouds.

Some nights,
we cannot see the
moon at all.
It has moved around
to the other side
of Earth.

19

IS THE MOON MADE OF CHEESE?

The moon is made of rock and dust.

Moon rock is grey and very hard. It is almost the same as rock found in volcanoes on Earth.

SOME BITS OF MOON ROCK ARE SPARKLY!

MOON ROCKS

You will need: 375 grams self-raising flour
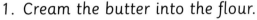
185 grams butter or margarine
185 grams sugar
125 grams coconut
1 egg
A little milk to mix

1. Cream the butter into the flour.
2. Add the sugar and coconut.
3. Mix in the beaten egg and milk.
4. Place in 'rocky heaps' on a greased baking sheet.
5. Ask an adult to help you bake them in an oven at 230°C for about 15 minutes until golden brown.

WHAT IS IT LIKE ON THE MOON?

There are mountains on the moon but no rivers or seas. The bare, rocky surface is covered with deep holes called craters.

Some craters are as big as 295 km wide and 4 km deep.

Most of the moon's craters were made when huge lumps of rock or stone came crashing through space and hit the moon.

WHOOSH!

CRASHING CRATERS!

Pour a pile of flour onto a tray.
Drop a ball into it from high above.

Lift the ball out carefully. You have made a crater!
(Do this outside — it can be very messy!)

23

IS THE MOON HOT OR COLD?

The moon gets very hot in the daytime. Heat from the Sun makes the moon hotter than boiling water.

THIS IS TOO HOT FOR ME!

BBRRR! IT'S F...F...FREEZING!

The moon gets very cold at night. Without heat from the Sun, the moon gets much colder than snow.

Astronauts need to wear spacesuits on the moon. Without them, they would burn up in the heat of the Sun or freeze in the cold shadows.

25

WHO LIVES ON THE MOON?

All people, animals and plants need air and water to live.

There is no air or water on the moon, so nothing grows there.
Nothing lives there.

MOON GARDENING

Cover a potted plant with a plastic bag. Secure it tightly with an elastic band so that no air gets in. Do not water the plant. What do you think will happen?

THE MOON MUST LOOK VERY GREY
WITHOUT TREES, GRASS OR FLOWERS!

Without air or water,
the plant soon wilts
and dies.

HAS ANYONE BEEN TO THE MOON?

In 1969, two astronauts from the USA landed on the moon. They were the first people to go there.
They brought many pieces of moon rock back to Earth.

The moon is airless. Astronauts have to take air with them so they can breathe on the moon.

THE FIRST PEOPLE WALKED ON THE MOON ON 20TH JULY, 1969!

The astronauts Neil Armstrong and Buzz Aldrin were the first people to land on the moon. Their footprints are still there. There is no rain or wind on the moon to wash or blow the footprints away.
They will be there forever.

29

GLOSSARY

astronaut Someone who travels in space.

crater A bowl-shaped hole made when one object crashes into another.

dinosaurs Reptiles that lived on Earth 65 million years ago.

Earth The planet we live on.

moon The ball of rock that orbits the Earth.

moonlight Light reflected from the Sun.

orbit The curved path of an object as it goes around a planet or star.

phases The different shapes of the moon.

space Space begins about 150 km away from the surface of Earth. It is full of planets and stars.

spacesuit A special suit worn by astronauts to protect them in space.

Sun A giant ball of burning gas that gives off light and heat.

wilt A plant droops and wilts when it is not watered enough or is dying.

INDEX